PREPARING FOR GAME DAY

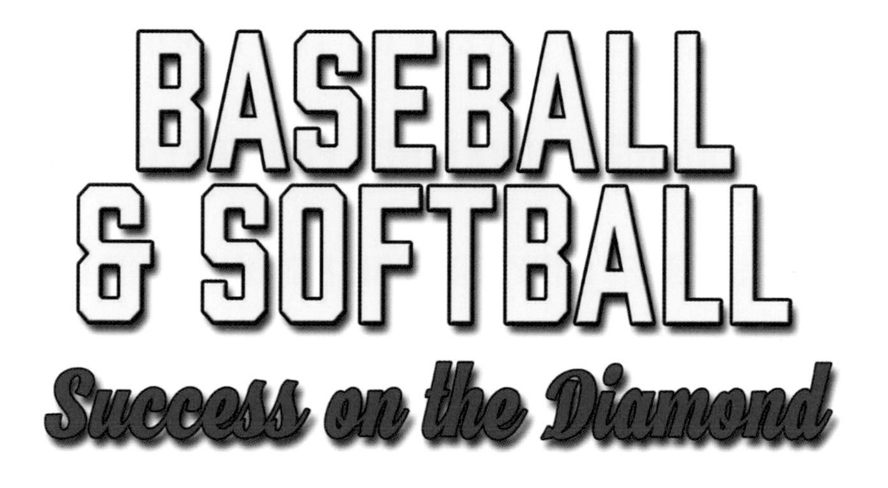

PREPARING FOR GAME DAY

BASEBALL & SOFTBALL: SUCCESS ON THE DIAMOND

BASKETBALL: STRATEGY ON THE HARDWOOD

CHEERLEADING: TECHNIQUES FOR PERFORMING

EXTREME SPORTS: POINTERS FOR PUSHING THE LIMITS

FOOTBALL: TOUGHNESS ON THE GRIDIRON

LACROSSE: FACING OFF ON THE FIELD

SOCCER: BREAKING AWAY ON THE PITCH

TRACK & FIELD: CONDITIONING FOR GREATNESS

VOLLEYBALL: APPROACHING THE NET

WRESTLING: CONTENDING ON THE MAT

PREPARING FOR GAME DAY

BASEBALL & SOFTBALL

Success on the Diamond

Peter Douglas

MASON CREST

Mason Crest
450 Parkway Drive, Suite D
Broomall, Pennsylvania 19008
(866) MCP-BOOK (toll free)

First printing
9 8 7 6 5 4 3 2 1

ISBN (hardback) 978-1-4222-3913-1
ISBN (series) 978-1-4222-3912-4
ISBN (ebook) 978-1-4222-7868-0

Cataloging-in-Publication Data on file with the Library of Congress

QR CODES AND LINKS TO THIRD-PARTY CONTENT

You may gain access to certain third-party content ("Third-Party Sites") by scanning and using the QR Codes that appear in this publication (the "QR Codes"). We do not operate or control in any respect any information, products, or services on such Third-Party Sites linked to by us via the QR Codes included in this publication, and we assume no responsibility for any materials you may access using the QR Codes. Your use of the QR Codes may be subject to terms, limitations, or restrictions set forth in the applicable terms of use or otherwise established by the owners of the Third-Party Sites. Our linking to such Third-Party Sites via the QR Codes does not imply an endorsement or sponsorship of such Third-Party Sites or the information, products, or services offered on or through the Third-Party Sites, nor does it imply an endorsement or sponsorship of this publication by the owners of such Third-Party Sites.

CONTENTS

KEY ICONS TO LOOK FOR:

Words to understand: These words with their easy-to-understand definitions will increase the reader's understanding of the text while building vocabulary skills.

Sidebars: This boxed material within the main text allows readers to build knowledge, gain insights, explore possibilities, and broaden their perspectives by weaving together additional information to provide realistic and holistic perspectives.

Educational Videos: Readers can view videos by scanning our QR codes, providing them with additional educational content to supplement the text. Examples include news coverage, moments in history, speeches, iconic sports moments and much more!

Text-dependent questions: These questions send the reader back to the text for more careful attention to the evidence presented there.

Research projects: Readers are pointed toward areas of further inquiry connected to each chapter. Suggestions are provided for projects that encourage deeper research and analysis.

Series glossary of key terms: This back-of-the book glossary contains terminology used throughout this series. Words found here increase the reader's ability to read and comprehend higher-level books and articles in this field.

WORDS TO UNDERSTAND:

adequate: enough for some need or requirement

static: exerting force by reason of weight alone without motion

tendencies: ways of behaving or proceeding that are developing and becoming more common

Chapter 1

GAME DAY

Baseball and softball do not require the same level of physical endurance that many other sports do. It is also very possible to be successful at these sports without being the biggest, strongest, or fastest athlete. Despite this, both sports still have physical elements players need to be ready for, and both require top-notch concentration in the field and at the plate. The following is a guideline on how to get ready before heading to the field and before stepping onto the diamond to play ball.

SLEEP WELL

Keeping a consistent sleep schedule will be an important part of every player's game day routine if they plan to be at their best. Eight hours of sleep is recommended the night before games. For professional players and others who travel, games might not end until 11 p.m., so many end up needing to sleep from 2 a.m. to 10 a.m. High school players are obviously in a different situation but need to be organized in their schedules to make sure they can prioritize the proper rest along with schoolwork and other obligations.

A solid fastball goes a long way. Kids don't really need to start messing around with all those pitches you see guys in the big leagues throwing. If you can locate a fastball, you can do a lot of damage as a pitcher.

— Pat Dean, Minnesota Twins pitcher

EAT WELL

With a good night's sleep accomplished, preparation to play continues immediately

A substantial high-protein breakfast is a good way to start game days.

after waking up. Breakfast will be the first step in providing the body the proper fuel it needs to perform well. A high protein choice like an egg-white omelet with vegetables and low-fat cheese is a good example of a healthy option. Carbs should be consumed in moderation for baseball and softball players. Oatmeal, some cereal, or a bagel in addition to the protein will provide about the right amount.

The next meal should occur about four hours after breakfast, as long as that is still more than two hours prior to game time. This should typically be the largest meal of the day for players, but remember, baseball and softball players do not need to eat extra calories, especially carbs, because the action is not continuous in these sports. A 180-lb. pitcher will burn about 450 calories an hour when he or she pitches. Fielders burn about 300. Compare this to basketball, tennis, volleyball, and hockey at 575, football at 650, or soccer at 740. Baseball and softball players just do not need to load up on calories and carbs. Starting pitchers might want to have a few more carbs at lunchtime before games in which they pitch but less on the other days when they do not play at all.

"The last thing I want is to be late to the bag. I always want to get there early. That's the pitcher's best friend, the double play. You always want to be able to make the double play. I gotta make sure I'm able to get to second base."

– Seven-time MLB All-Star 2B Robinson Canó

In general, baseball and softball players should eat about 2.7 grams (0.1 ounces) of carbs per pound (0.5 kilograms) of body weight each day. Protein intake should be about 0.8 grams (0.03 ounces) per pound, with fat at 0.5 grams (0.02 ounces) per pound each day.

A good lunch would therefore include lean protein like fish or chicken breast, low-fat milk, cheese, or yogurt with some bread, fruit, and nuts. An example would be a turkey sandwich or burger with lettuce, tomato, and low-fat Swiss cheese on whole grain bread with plain Greek yogurt mixed with berries and a small salad.

Around midafternoon, sports nutritionists like Kate Patton of the Cleveland Indians recommend a protein-packed snack like a yogurt smoothie. Typically this would be immediately prior to batting practice (BP) for the team. After BP and between one and two hours before the first pitch should come the final pregame meal. This last meal should provide more protein and some carbs, but avoid vegetables and fat. Chicken and rice with some fruit is an example of what Patton would recommend to players.

A Major League Baseball (MLB) game lasts about three hours. High school and college games will typically be shorter, but even so, it will have been three to five hours since the pregame meal, which means after the game, it is time to eat again. Recovery assistance is a goal with this meal. Fish, rice, vegetables, and fruit are good options. To aid in recovery, a sixteen-ounce protein shake before going to sleep will help with muscle repair.

"With a man on first base, you'd preferably like to bunt the ball to first base. You want to set your bat angle early. If you're left-handed, set it at the shortstop. If you're right-handed, set it at the second baseman."

– Juan Pierre,
2003 World Series champion

Lunch should be a player's biggest meal on game days and should include protein and carbs.

"Hold the ball with your index finger and thumb going with the horseshoe. Grip is somewhat personal. If you can get correct spin with a different grip, then use it. Whichever grip you choose, make sure it results in four seam rotation."

– Cat Osterman, 2004 USA Softball Olympic gold medalist

WARM-UP

As important as it is to put fuel in the tank, it is equally as important to oil the parts. A warm engine runs more smoothly, and the same goes for the body.

A traditional baseball or softball warm-up involves **static** stretches and short sprints to help get the body ready for the movements it will be undergoing in the game. This stretching is done ahead of fielding, throwing, and BP.

Pros discuss pregame hitting drills.

Players will then usually do some final warm-up exercises, such as arm circles, to get ready for the action to come. Experts recommend taking the traditional warm-up another step further by incorporating some dynamic movements geared specifically toward baseball movements. This is useful as it gradually prepares the muscles for baseball-specific movements while decreasing the chance of injury and enhancing strength, flexibility, and power. And unlike static stretching, dynamic warm-up exercises increase rather than decrease motor function.

Warm-up exercises could include ones like these, suggested by Livestrong.com:

Throwing the ball back and forth with teammates is part of a traditional baseball or softball warm-up.

SPRINTS

The first thing that should be done in a warm-up is five to ten short sprints that simulate the action you would see in a game. This will get the body's core temperature warmed up, and it will also increase circulation to the muscles. Start at the first base line. Sprint to second base, walk back, and sprint again.

FORWARD BENDS

Stand in a wide stance with your arms out to your sides and parallel to the ground. Bend forward, and touch your right hand to your left foot. Come back up, and then touch your left hand to your right foot. Alternate back and forth three to six times.

ROTATIONS

Trunk rotations are done with your feet in a wide stance and your hands extended out to your sides and parallel to the ground. Rotate your upper body to the right, then rotate it to the left. Every time you rotate, try to go a little bit further. Go back and forth three to six times.

"I throw my slider as a strikeout pitch or a pitch early in the count if there's a guy who's going to be potentially swinging first pitch, or a guy who's just bad at swinging on breaking balls."

– Garrett Richards,
Los Angeles Angels pitcher

Squats help softball players stretch out their quads and hamstrings before a workout.

"Box up the lower half of the pitcher's body from the back of the kneecaps to the heels in a little rectangle. You're going to be able to see that front foot go up and that back heel come off the rubber in a pick situation. That's our visual. We're really shrinking our focus."

– Rich Hill, University of San Diego head coach

KNEE LIFTS

Knee lifts loosen up the legs and hip flexors. To do these, stand with your feet about shoulder width apart. Lift your right foot off the ground, and bring your knee up to your chest. Lower it back down, and bring your left knee up. Go back and forth three to six times. You can also do these in a walking motion.

SQUATS

Squats loosen up the glutes, quads, and hamstrings. To do these, stand with your feet about shoulder width apart. Bend your knees, and lower your body slowly until your thighs are parallel to the ground, then stand back up. Go up in a fast and controlled motion. Do three to six reps.

WALKING LUNGES

To do walking lunges, take a long step forward with your right foot. Bend down until your front knee is ninety degrees and your back knee is about two inches (five centimeters) off the ground. Come back up, step forward with your left leg, and follow the same procedure three to six times.

DROP LUNGES

Drop lunges are done to loosen up the hips. Start with your feet together, and place your hands in front of your body like you are boxing. Step back behind your body at an angle with your left foot. Come into a squat, come up, and bring your foot back to the starting point. Step back behind your body at an angle with your right foot. Come into a squat, and come back to the starting position. Go back and forth three to six times.

CROSSES

Arm crosses help loosen up the chest and rear shoulders. Stand with your feet about shoulder width apart and your arms out to your sides with your palms down. Extend your arms behind you, and then cross them in front of your body. Go back and forth three to six times, then turn your palms up and repeat.

CIRCLES

Arm circles are another stretch that loosens up the shoulders. Stand with your feet about shoulder width apart. Extend your arms out straight to your sides, and make small circles in both directions. Do three to six small circles, then repeat with medium-size circles and large circles.

"When leading off from second base, always make eye contact with the catcher. Make sure that you're telling him you are a good base runner, a great base stealer and you're paying attention."

– John Cangelosi, 1997 World Series champion

STRETCHES

- Sit with your legs outstretched. Bend the knee on the right leg to bring the sole of the right foot against the left thigh. Take hold of the leg just above the ankle, while you rotate the ankle. Rotate for thirty seconds, and repeat on the left side. This will help avoid ankle sprains.
- Sit with your legs outstretched, and then reach forward on the right side to grasp your ankle or toes. Hold for thirty seconds. Repeat three times on each side. This will help prevent hamstring pulls or sprains.
- From a standing position, bend at the knees, return to standing, then touch your toes. Do ten repetitions. These exercises will help you avoid back and thigh injuries.

"There are not two different swings. You don't swing down on a rise ball and swing under a drop ball. That's a fallacy. It's incorrect. We should have one swing."

– Sue Enquist, eleven-time national softball champion coach

> “The first thing you’ve got to do when you see a pop-up is take your mask off. Keep it in your hand, and locate the ball. Then you throw the mask away from you.”

– Miguel Montero, 2016 World Series champion and two-time All-Star MLB catcher

On hot, humid days, players need to be sure to stay well hydrated.

KEEP DRINKING

During all of the eating and warming up going on throughout game day, players must be sure to keep themselves well hydrated along the way. The body needs water to perform optimally, not just physically but mentally as well. Typically, the body will tell you when your fluids are getting low by activating its thirst mechanism. In ordinary day-to-day life, listening to your body will work just fine to maintain **adequate** hydration. For athletes, however, hydration needs to be more than simply adequate. Those needs should be optimally met. Therefore, athletes should not wait to feel thirsty before drinking something. On game day, hydration should be part of the routine.

Be sure to consider your fluid needs throughout the day, starting at breakfast with eight ounces of either water or low-fat milk. Drink another eight ounces around mid-morning, choosing water or perhaps a low-calorie sports drink. Eight more ounces of water should accompany the lunchtime meal, and two hours before the game starts, or right after batting practice, drink sixteen ounces of water or a low-calorie sports drink.

There is no clock in baseball or softball, so there is no set amount you should drink during a game as they vary in length. The best rule of thumb is to try to drink between four and eight ounces while in the dugout during your team’s at bat each inning. This should be on the higher side during hot and humid days when players are losing a lot of fluid from excessive sweating. This is the optimal time to incorporate a low-calorie sports drink to help replenish nutrients lost in the heat.

Hydration is important postgame as well. Especially on hot days, players can lose a few pounds during a game due to fluid loss. Weigh yourself before and after games, and force yourself to drink twenty-four ounces of water for every pound that was lost.

Adopting this kind of fluid schedule will not only keep the body in peak performance mode, but it will also help to prevent muscle cramps and, more seriously, heat stroke.

Little League softball players warm up before a game in Nevada.

HEAD GAMES

It is game day, and you have done everything possible to get your body ready to play. You have had plenty of sleep, eaten a well-balanced diet, and topped up your energy reserves. Your muscles are warm and loose, and your body is a well-hydrated machine. Great, your body is prepared. But will you know what to tell it to do when you get out on the diamond? Do you know what the other team's starter relies on as an out pitch in a given situation? Do you know which opponent is likely to steal a base, and what count the other team likes to try to steal on? These questions and dozens more like them are all ones you should have answers to if you are mentally prepared to play every game.

"You're going to want to choke up on the bat as your back foot is coming forward. The amount you want to choke up on the bat depends on if you want to do a soft slap or a hard slap. The more you choke up, the softer it's going to be."

– Jessica Mendoza, 2004 Olympic gold medalist outfielder

First of all, make sure you know your team's signs. There is a lot of nonverbal communication in baseball, and not knowing a sign can lead to a crucial error that costs your team the game and earns you a spot on the bench. Pay attention out there. Players

Baseball and softball have long periods of inactivity for some players and require far less endurance than many other sports.

should be concentrating all the time in the field and at the plate. You do not want to be that second baseman who misses the pitchout and watches your catcher toss the ball into center field, helping the runner to score instead of being picked off.

Players should always know the **tendencies** of the pitchers in the game on both teams. As a fielder, you should know what your pitcher likes to throw and whether the pitch is more likely to result in a ground ball or fly ball. Know how to position yourself according to the most likely outcome of any given situation. For example, if your left-handed pitcher is facing a right-handed batter, the hitter may have a tough time getting around on the pitch, and the ball is more likely to be hit up the middle. This is the kind of thing a mentally prepared player will know. You should also know the opposing starter's best pitches and what he or she is likely to throw in a given count.

Players should also know the tendencies of the hitters in the game as well. Knowing your own team's hitters can help you on the base paths, while knowing the opposition hitters can help you in the field. Among other things that your coach will focus on in practice, you should know which players are likely to bunt in given situations, who the other coach is likely to hit and run with, and how fast each of their players is, so you know how much time you have to field a ground ball. Learning what players tend to do, on average, in a given situation, will help you anticipate plays. That mental advantage could give you the split second you need to make the play.

TEXT-DEPENDENT QUESTIONS:

1. What should typically be the largest meal of the day for players?

2. Warm-ups involve what kind of stretches and short sprints to help get the body ready for the movements it will be undergoing in the game?

3. How many ounces of water or other forms of healthy drinks should an athlete consume on game day?

RESEARCH PROJECT:

Put together a scouting report on the pitchers on your team if you are a position player or on the hitters if you pitch. Document their tendencies in all situations to make it as predictive as possible.

WORDS TO UNDERSTAND:

propelled: driven forward or onward by or as if by means of a force that imparts motion

resin: a yellowish or brownish substance obtained from the gum or sap of some trees (such as the pine) and used in varnishes

susceptible: easily affected, influenced, or harmed by something

Chapter 2

THINK THE GAME

IMAGERY

A positive and confident mind-set is a key to success for any athlete. If you are convinced that you are prepared, and you are confident of winning, the game is almost won. We all can tell when a team is "up" for a game, being inspired to play better than normal. Perhaps their motivation comes from the fact that this is a crucial contest, or they wish to avenge a previous defeat or win for a retiring coach. Whatever the reason, the players are mentally fired up.

Players using the technique known as imagery rehearse in their minds positive plays such as sliding into a base safely.

This type of mental conditioning can be very effective in baseball and softball. The technique known as imagery helps reduce nervousness and increase confidence. If you are a pitcher who will be facing a dangerous batter, for instance, you can visualize striking out your opponent with a clever mixture of your best pitches. You can imagine what the ball feels like coming off your fingertips with the perfect rotation, and imagine hearing the thump of the ball hitting the catcher's mitt as the batter swings and misses. Rehearse in your mind the times that you have slid safely into home plate, handled a line drive in the infield, or leaped and thrown over a runner at second to complete a double play. Remember that you can build up a positive self-image by controlling your attitudes and emotions.

Some experts believe that negative thinking makes athletes more **susceptible** to getting injured. If you control anxiety and anger, you will play better and safer. This is so important that professional baseball teams have sports psychologists on their staffs who work with players on mental conditioning. Most non-Major League players, of course, do not have such professional help and must rely on themselves and on pep talks with other team members to learn how to relax, gain confidence, reduce stress, and avoid injuries. This is where imagery becomes even more important.

Find a time and place to relax, then picture yourself in a game, remembering the way the stadium looks and the views and sounds that you will experience from your position on the field: the grass, the bullpen, the scoreboard, the dugout chatter, even the fans roaring their approval at your play. Imagine hitting a home run into the bleachers, stealing a base, or catching a fly ball against the outfield fence to retire the team at bat.

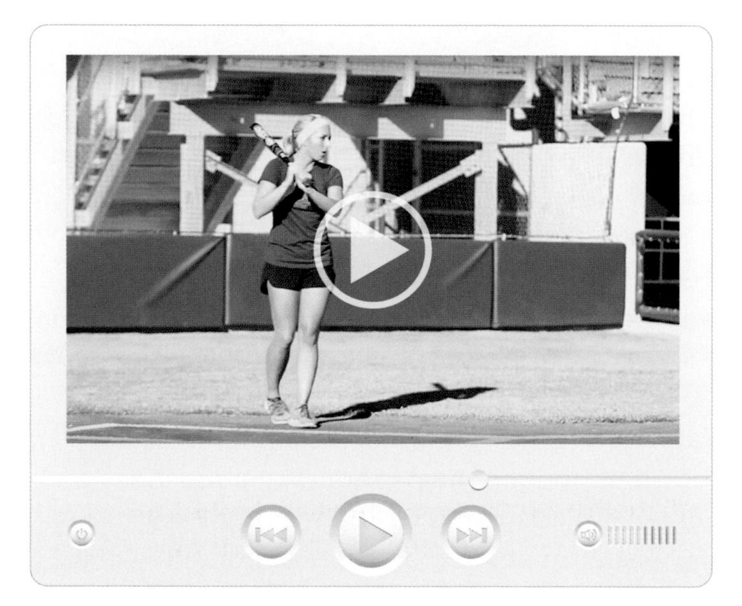

Texas A&M two-time All-American Amanda Scarborough talks about the mental approach to an at bat.

CONCENTRATION

Concentration is another key component of making the correct play, which in turn leads to reduced mistakes and reduced chance of injury. Whether batting or playing defense, you can be both "psyched up" and calm at the same time. This "relaxed attention" can be increased by talking to yourself: "Here comes the fastball," "Watch out for the bunt," "He'll be running on the

As the closest player in the path of a hard-hit ball, the pitcher must be mentally alert after every pitch.

next pitch," and so on. There is usually relaxed chatter among the infield players as they encourage each other. Good players enjoy the competition and are not too anxious or tense about their batting and fielding. They know that it is not the end of the world if they strike out or commit an error. Many more opportunities will come to a well-trained player.

GEAR UP

Being mentally alert, concentrating, and being confident are all good tools in establishing a mind-set that leads to the proper decisions and reduces the chance of getting injured. Physically, however, the best way to have a safe game is obviously to wear protective equipment. In a recent report on sports injuries by the U.S. Consumer Product Safety Commission (CPSC), more than 190,000 baseball and softball injuries were treated in U.S. emergency rooms in players age five to fourteen. The CPSC also estimates that more than 58,000 baseball injuries to children, or nearly 36 percent of all baseball injuries, would be prevented or reduced by wearing proper protective equipment.

In both baseball and softball, being struck by a thrown or batted ball is the major hazard. Do not be fooled by the name. A softball does not feel soft when it hits you traveling at a hundred miles an hour. Many injuries to young players from a batted, pitched, or thrown ball are due to the player's unskilled response. The standard baseball is made of a core of cork or rubber, which is wound with fibers, such as cotton or wool, and then covered with two pieces of leather sewn together with 108 stitches. It can be pitched at more than ninety miles per hour (145 kilometers per hour), so hard that helmets are required for batters in organized leagues. And when hit strongly with a high-tech aluminum bat, the ball may be **propelled** at far more than one hundred miles per hour (160 kilometers per hour), so all defensive players must always wear gloves.

It may not be as hard as a baseball, but when thrown or hit by a bat, a softball does not feel very soft.

As the closest player in the path of a well-hit ball, the pitcher is in the most vulnerable position, but being hit by a line drive is a possibility for any infielder. Pitchers, however, have the least amount of time to protect themselves. Infielders must remain alert at all times and be aware of every time a pitch is being thrown. There is a lot of time between pitches, and it can be easy to get distracted. For pitchers, they should practice getting into a defensive position following every delivery instead of relying on a quick reaction to the outcome of the pitch.

CATCHERS

On a pitch-by-pitch basis, the catcher occupies the most dangerous position on the field and therefore wears the most protective equipment. Otherwise, he or she would be injured by foul balls or a wrongly swung bat. The gear is jokingly called the "tools of ignorance," implying that the user would have to be pretty ignorant of the potential consequences to volunteer for a job that required this much protection. As well as the mitt, the catcher's protection should include a helmet, face mask, chest protector, throat protector, shin guards, and a protective supporter cup. All this may look like a burden, but modern equipment is lightweight and provides good freedom of movement.

Catcher gear consists of a helmet and mask with a throat protector, a chest protector, shin guards, and a padded mitt.

Typically, each catcher will catch about 150 pitches in each nine-inning game. The leather catcher's mitt, therefore, is vital for protecting hands and fingers. It should always be worn during practice sessions and warm-ups. The mitt has extra padding and is 15.5 inches (39 centimeters) from top to bottom, which is 3.5 inches (9 centimeters) longer than a fielder's glove. Amateur players should never use a fielder's glove if they are playing catcher.

Like the catcher, the home plate umpire also wears a mask for protection from foul balls.

The most vital part of a catcher's gear is the mask and helmet as they protect the head and face. Modern versions of this headgear are strong but lightweight. A helmet usually has vinyl on the outside and leather inside. The masks have a steel framework, and some newer ones are made of a new **resin** compound advertised to be stronger than steel. Both versions of the mask can be flipped up. The mask is on properly when it is squarely over the face and tightened with the adjustable straps. Individual "goat's beard" throat protectors can be attached to hang from the bottom, but many masks have a built-in wire extension that is two inches (five centimeters) long. Some have side deflectors built in for extra ear protection. As with the glove, helmets and masks should always be worn during a practice or warm-up as well as for games.

A long, padded chest protector covers catchers in several key areas: upper chest, abdomen, groin, collarbone, and lower neck. They also wear shin guards, which should fit perfectly over the lower legs to protect from bruises, so catchers wear their baseball shoes when choosing guards to make sure they are the correct length. A shin guard should cover the kneecap, shinbone, and lower leg and should also have wings to protect the ankle and foot. Most versions add an extended instep plate.

HITTERS, FIELDERS, AND CALLING BALLS AND STRIKES

Since he or she stands directly behind the catcher to get the best view to

Many youth leagues mandate the use of helmets that offer facial protection.

call balls and strikes, the plate umpire is also heavily protected. This includes a padded body protector, now normally worn underneath the shirt, which covers the chest, shoulders, and upper arms. The umpire's mask needs to provide protection to the side of the head and the throat. It should also offer excellent visibility, enabling the umpire to make accurate decisions.

Batting helmets made their first appearance in 1938. Today, batters are required to wear them. The hard plastic shell has foam padding inside and extends to cover the ears. The helmet should fit snugly on the head without the back rim resting on the neck, and the bill should not be too low on the forehead because that would block the player's vision. Ordinary baseball caps should not be worn under helmets.

At most levels of baseball and softball, the helmet is worn on its own, leaving the face exposed. Youth baseball and softball players have more face, eye, and mouth injuries than players in any other sport. Safer versions of helmets are available and include either a wire face mask or a transparent plastic shield to cover the face from the tip of the nose to below the chin. This extra protection for the face is required by some youth baseball organizations. Batters can also add plastic goggles, custom-fitted mouth guards, forearm and wrist guards, ankle guards, and shock absorbers worn over the second and middle fingers.

FIELDERS' GLOVES

There are different fielders' gloves for different positions. Infielders' gloves are slightly smaller than those of the outfielders because of the quick play required, but the first baseman has a longer webbing to snag fast throws. Fielders can also protect their eyes by wearing sports goggles.

OTHER SAFETY EQUIPMENT

One fun aspect of baseball for kids is sliding into a base. That fun comes with a cost, however, as every year, more than 6,600 players are injured in this way. A safety-release base may help prevent the injuries caused in organized play when younger players slide into bases. The safety-release base is anchored to rubber mats, and if it receives hard contact, it will pop away, leaving no parts sticking out of the ground and no holes in the ground.

Baseball players may be the most superstitious of any athletes in any sport. Here are five examples.

1. Pitcher John Wetteland refused to wear different caps during the season. He had the one he wore opening day and stuck with it no matter what. In 1996, when his New York Yankee team made the World Series, he refused to wear the new hat with the World Series logo. Instead, he had the logo sewed on to his faded, sweat-stained hat.

2. Hall of Famer Stan Musial was one of baseball's best players in the 1940s and 1950s. Musial was very particular about his breakfast on game days. He always ate the same thing in the same order: one egg, followed by two pancakes, followed by a second egg.

3. All-Star center fielder Lenny Dykstra blamed his failings at the plate on his batting gloves. Every time he made an out in a game, he would throw out the batting gloves he was wearing. He kept a supply of gloves handy and wore new ones in his next at bat.

4. Pitcher Don Robinson could obviously catch a baseball, but he just did not want to, at least not to start an inning on the mound. He insisted on picking the ball up off the ground. If someone did throw him the ball, he would let it fall and come to rest and then pick it up.

5. Pitcher Turk Wendell was a little superstitious about the number nine. He believed it was his lucky number, and he couldn't have enough nines. He wore number ninety-nine on his uniform for three different teams. In 2000, he signed a contract in the amount of $9,999,999.99.

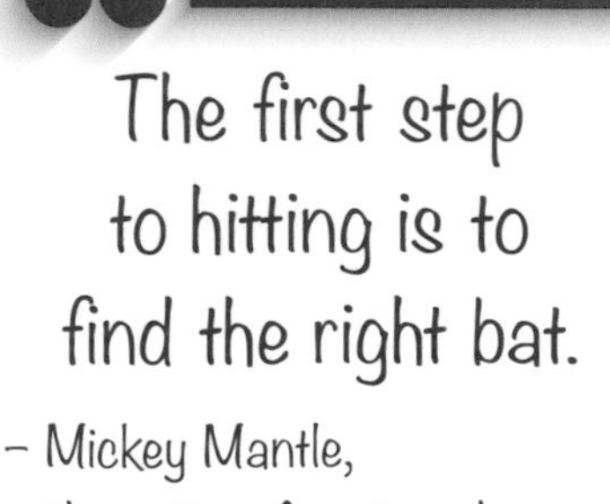

The first of the famous Louisville Slugger bats was made in this factory in 1884.

BASEBALL BATS

Baseball and softball bats come in many different sizes and materials, giving players a lot of choices. The famous Louisville Slugger was first made in 1884, and in 2003 the company produced 1.4 million of them for professional and amateur players.

Professional teams must use wooden bats, which are shaped, sanded, and given a natural or flame-burned finish. These have traditionally been made of white ash, but recent years have seen a trend toward maple or a combination of the two. Maple bats do not break as easily, and they hit further. More than three-quarters of MLB players now use maple bats.

Light and long-hitting aluminum bats were first used in 1971 and have been popular since the 1980s with teams in youth leagues, high schools, and colleges. If professionals switched to them, however, players would score so many home runs that the stadiums would have to be expanded.

Most MLB players now use maple bats, which do not break as easily as traditional ash bats.

TEXT-DEPENDENT QUESTIONS:

1. Professional baseball teams have sports psychologists on their staffs who work with players on what?

2. The U.S. CPSC estimates that more than 58,000 baseball injuries to children would be prevented or reduced by wearing what?

3. In what year was the famous Louisville Slugger first made?

RESEARCH PROJECT:

Aluminum bats have been around for decades. How much have they changed baseball and softball since they were introduced? Research how hitting and power numbers were affected when metal took over from wood.

WORDS TO UNDERSTAND:

rotator cuff: a group of muscles and tendons that are around your shoulder and that allow it to move in all directions

trudging: walking slowly and heavily because you are tired or working very hard

velocity: quickness of motion

Chapter 3

TRAIN FOR SUCCESS

WARMING UP

Warming up before practice or workouts is one of the best ways to prevent baseball or softball injuries because cold muscles are more likely to be injured, and stiff muscles cause clumsy play. Increased flexibility will make it easier for you to respond more quickly in a game. Besides warming the muscles, warm-up exercises will stretch them as well as the ligaments and other connective tissues. Such exercises are also aerobic, so your heart and breathing rates will also increase, supplying additional oxygen to your body's system. Even a warm-up of five to ten minutes will have a positive effect. This could include simple walking or running in place, followed by jumping jacks. We've all seen players warming up at their positions on the field: players making relaxed throws around the infield, pitchers tossing the ball in the bullpen, and upcoming batters swinging in the on-deck circle.

Warming up before practice will loosen muscles and ligaments, allowing for quicker responses during play.

Players should focus on stretching the muscles that will get the most use in whatever practice or workout they are preparing for. Throwing is the movement most used in the games of baseball and softball; pitchers, catchers, infielders, and outfielders must all protect their throwing arms. To help avoid sore arms and injuries, try these stretching exercises:

- Let one arm hang loosely next to the body. Then take the elbow with your other hand and pull the arm until the biceps touch your chin. Hold for five to ten seconds. Then change arms and repeat. Do this two or three times for each arm.
- Place one arm on the back of your head, then put your other hand on the top of the elbow, and pull it lightly for five to ten seconds. Switch arms and repeat. Again, do this two or three times for each arm.

Throwing is also the most common pregame warm-up done on the field:

Two players stand twenty-five to forty feet (eight to twelve meters) apart and toss the ball back and forth about a dozen times. Use a big circle movement of the arm to stretch the shoulder and **rotator cuff**. Increase the distance to forty-five to sixty-five feet (fourteen to twenty meters) for about ten throws. Players who are twelve years old or younger should not throw at this longer distance, which might cause injuries.

Prior to a game starting, pitchers should work off the bullpen mound, or any set distance no longer than their regular pitches during a game, and throw fifteen to twenty-five pitches. It is important to limit the number and types of pitches thrown by a young pitcher. Serious injuries can occur to a player's growth plates, where bone growth occurs near the joints. Too much stress placed on the elbow and shoulder can cause damage, even a chipped bone, which would ruin the possibility of a baseball career. Little League puts pitch limits on its players.

Starting pitchers typically warm up their arms by throwing in the bullpen prior to games.

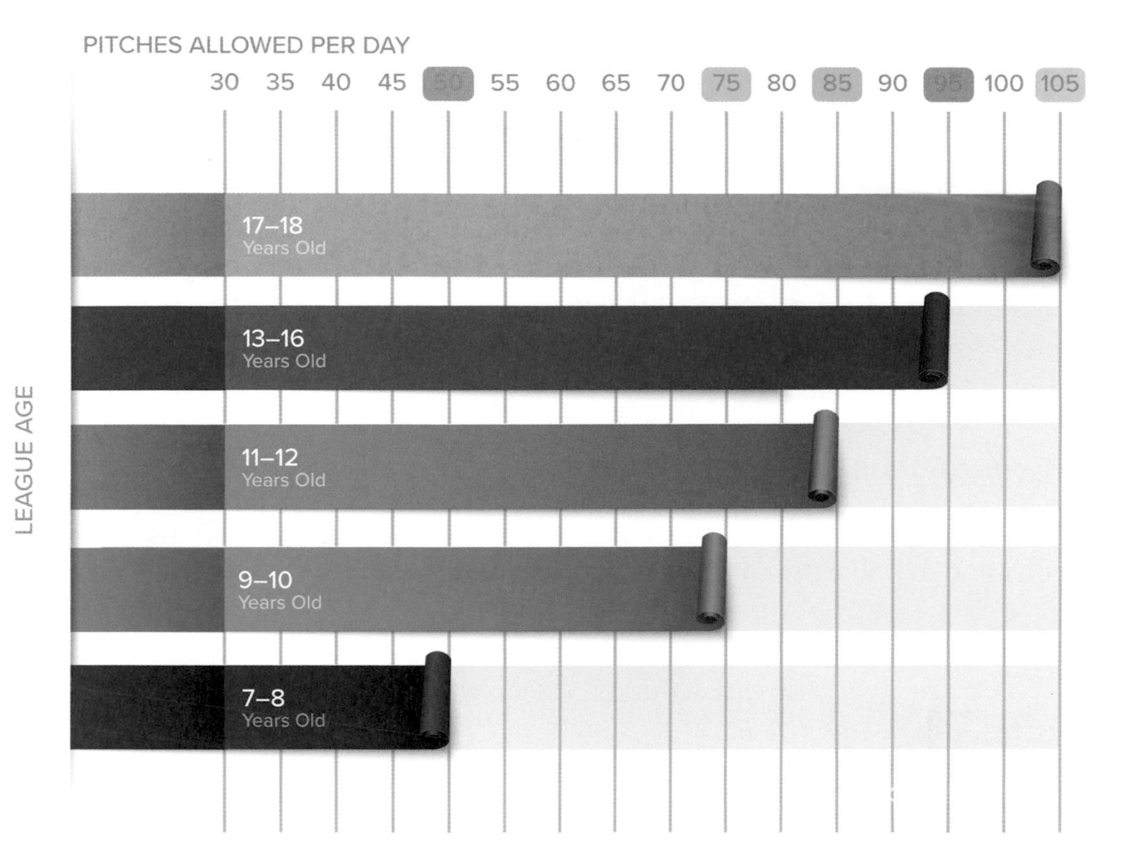

Each league must designate a scorekeeper or official to track pitch counts as the official pitch-count recorder. The pitch-count recorder must provide the current pitch count for any pitcher when requested by either manager or any umpire and notify the umpire in chief when a pitcher has reached the pitch limit. The umpire in chief must then notify the pitcher's manager that the pitcher must be removed. Failure of the pitch-count recorder to notify the umpire in chief and/or the failure of the umpire in chief to notify the manager does not relieve the manager of his or her responsibility to remove the pitcher when that pitcher is no longer eligible to pitch. Violation of the rule can result in a protest of the game in which it occurs.

Young pitchers need to follow strict pitch counts to protect their developing arms.

Here are a few examples of plyometric exercises designed to enhance baseball-specific upper body strength.

Upper Body Plyometric Exercises for Baseball

Plyometric Push-Ups

These plyometric exercises are designed to build explosiveness in the upper body and to make the traditional push-up movement much more difficult.

Clap Push-Up

1. Acquire the normal push-up position.
2. Perform the typical negative portion of a push-up.
3. On the positive portion, you will literally push up off the ground.
4. Your hands and upper body should be in the air.
5. Land softly, and transition right back into the negative portion.
6. There is no rest between each repetition. Perform this exercise eight to ten times.

Stability Ball Clap Push-Up

This is the same as the previous exercise, except your feet will be balanced on a stability ball. This increases the level of difficulty.

One-Arm Plyo Push-Up

You will need a small medicine ball for this exercise. One hand will balance on the ball, and the other will be on the ground. Go to the push-up position, then forcefully explode upward, and repeat.

The American Sports Medicine Institute (ASMI) has its own guidelines for young pitchers.

1. Watch and respond to signs of fatigue (such as decreased ball **velocity**, decreased accuracy, upright trunk during pitching, dropped elbow during pitching, or increased time between pitches). If an adolescent pitcher complains of fatigue or looks fatigued, let him or her rest from pitching and other throwing.
2. There should be no overhead throwing of any kind for at least two to three months per year (four months is preferred). There should be no competitive baseball pitching for at least four months per year.
3. Do not pitch more than one hundred innings in games in any calendar year.
4. Follow limits for pitch counts and days of rest.
5. Avoid pitching on multiple teams with overlapping seasons.
6. Learn good throwing mechanics as soon as possible. The first steps should be to learn in order: 1) basic throwing, 2) fastball pitching, 3) change-up pitching.
7. Avoid using radar guns.
8. A pitcher should not also be a catcher for his team. The pitcher-catcher combination results in many throws and may increase the risk of injury.
9. If a pitcher complains of pain in his or her elbow or shoulder, discontinue pitching until evaluated by a sports medicine physician. Inspire adolescent pitchers to have fun playing baseball and other sports. Participation and enjoyment of various physical activities will increase the player's athleticism and interest in sports.

The limits referred to in point four are as follows:

WEEKLY LIMITS

7-14 yrs. old:

21-35 pitches = 1 day rest

36-50 pitches = 2 days rest

51-65 pitches = 3 days rest

66+ pitches = 4 days rest

15-18 yrs. old:

31-45 pitches = 1 day rest

46-60 pitches = 2 days rest

61-75 pitches = 3 days rest

76+ pitches = 4 days rest

Curveballs should not be thrown in any quantity by pitchers under twelve years old. These types of pitches involve a snapping motion of the wrist and put pressure on the arm, all of which could cause serious damage.

There are a lot of routine actions in baseball and softball that require repeating the same motions over and over. Think of a shortstop who constantly cuts off ground balls and turns quickly to throw them to first or a batter swinging at pitches, always from the same side of the plate. Repeating these moves over and over can cause rotational strains and pains. These can be minimized by a warm-up that includes a few light rotation moves.

Pitches like the curveball put a lot of pressure on the joints of the arm and should not be thrown by pitchers who are still growing.

Baseball and softball are games with a lot of down time between periods of activity. Walking around a bit is better than sitting out a long half inning. Also, players should briskly jog back onto the field rather than **trudging** back to their positions. These small efforts will help to keep players lively and alert when this is needed in the late innings. After a game, players should also do light walking and stretching to help the heart and body gradually slow down.

THE IMPORTANCE OF FLEXIBILITY

Kevin Pillar of the Toronto Blue Jays stretches by doing trunk rotations before batting practice.

In both baseball and softball, it helps players to be strong and also to be fast. Modern professional baseball is filled with fast and explosive plays, and anyone who cannot perform these tasks instantly is sure to be left behind. Because of this, players often perform the same motion repeatedly or stay in a certain position, such as a shortstop twisting to throw to first base often or a catcher holding his mitt in the same position throughout the game. Doing the same thing over and over like this decreases the flexibility of your muscles. If this happens, sudden or strong movements outside the usual range of motion can cause injuries such as ligament or tendon tears. Here are a few stretches that you should do before and after every practice and workout to keep these joints flexible and to decrease the risk of injury:

- Lie on your back, bend your knees, and let them fall to one side. Keep your arms out straight to either side of you, and let your back and hips rotate with your knees.
- Stick one arm straight out in front of you. Rotate your wrist down and outward, and then use your other hand to gently continue to rotate your hand upward.
- Stand up straight, and place your hand behind the middle of your back with your elbow pointing straight out to your side. With your other hand, reach over and gently pull your elbow forward.

PHYSICAL CONDITIONING

Overuse injuries caused by repetitive stress on body parts are common in baseball and softball. A regular physical conditioning program throughout the year (not just during baseball season) will provide additional protection against these and other injuries. This program can be a combination of running, swimming, cycling, and other exercises, such as push-ups, pull-ups, and sit-ups. Aerobic conditioning is needed to avoid fatigue, and strength and endurance training can help reduce injury and also promote health. Good strenuous physical activity for twenty to thirty minutes, three days a week, will greatly improve a player's endurance.

Heavy strength training, especially weight training, and even resistance training and plyometrics as well, should be avoided by young players. All players, no matter their age, need to avoid too much training as the baseball and softball seasons approach. Training that is too long or too vigorous can lead to extra tiredness, stress, and poor performance on the field.

WEIGHT TRAINING

Increased muscle strength is the goal of weight training. There are two common types of equipment used to achieve this. The first is free weights or barbells, which consist of weighted disks placed on a bar that is lifted by the athlete. The other types of equipment used in weight training are weight machines, which use weights placed on sliders or cables that a person must then push or pull to move. Weight machines tend to be safer than free weights because it is impossible to drop the weights on yourself, and they are specifically designed to exercise one muscle or group of muscles at a time. By lifting the same amount of weight many times and gradually over time increasing the amount lifted, an athlete can strengthen his or her muscles.

Strength is an asset in baseball and softball. Stronger players can throw and swing harder. However, it is easy to strain yourself during weight training by attempting to lift more than you can handle. When starting a new weight-lifting routine, you will be exercising muscles that have likely never been used very much before. Overusing these muscles can lead to serious injury. Also, there is always the danger of dropping a weight on yourself, no matter how experienced you are. For these reasons, no new weight-lifting regimen should be started without consulting an expert, and you should never lift weights without someone else nearby to help you. Also, weight training has negative effects on the developing skeletons of young people. When you have not finished growing, weight training wears down the growth plates on your bones, which keeps your bones from growing fully and results in stunted growth. Therefore, if you are under seventeen, you should not begin a weight-training regimen.

Players at the University of California-Berkley work on strength and conditioning.

Resistance bands put much less stress on joints and bones than traditional weight training.

RESISTANCE TRAINING

Players can also increase strength through resistance training. Resistance training is working against some force other than gravity. An example of this is the use of resistance bands. The shorter the band, the greater the resistance. The benefits of resistance training are many and include increased muscle strength and size as well as greater bone density. Unlike weights, bands do not put the same kind of stress on joints and bones and instead help to strengthen them. Studies have shown that resistance training has decreased the frequency not only of joint injuries but of lower back injuries and muscle strains as well.

Despite its many, many positive effects, athletes should still take care not to strain themselves with any new resistance training program. As with any new regimen, an expert should be consulted beforehand, and you should ease into your new program to allow your body to adapt to the new stresses and to avoid unnecessary strain.

> ***During the year, I like to maintain my strength and not work out too much weight. A lot of band work, medicine ball, ab work, just maintaining that strength. In the off-season, it's mainly heavy weight and just trying to build that strength up for the year.***
>
> ***– Mike Trout, two-time American League MVP outfielder***

PLYOMETRICS

Explosiveness, which is the power to make strength moves quickly, is another characteristic that helps baseball and softball players. They can use plyometrics to build this power. Plyometrics are high-intensity exercises with many exaggerated motions. The principle behind plyometrics is that when you stretch a muscle before it has a chance to contract, it contracts with more force than usual, which improves muscle tone and strength as well as flexibility. Some examples of plyometric exercises include:

- Jump from a small box, and rebound off of the floor onto a higher box.
- Stand with one foot in front of the other. With your front knee behind the toe, bend into a lunge. Jump up, and switch your legs in midair, landing in a lunge with the opposite foot in front.
- Place your feet together. Bend your knees until you are squatting, and jump as high as you can. Land in a squatting position, and repeat this for up to one minute.

As with any technique, plyometrics must be performed properly to reduce the risk of getting hurt. Most of the injuries sustained during plyometrics are due to bad form. For example, landing the wrong way on your foot over and over again can gradually strain your foot until injury is inevitable. That is why you should always have an expert teach you the correct form for plyometric exercises. Attempting plyometrics without any strength training can also result in overstraining the muscles because most plyometric exercises take advantage of gravity to put a greater load on your body than usual. As with all new exercise programs, you should ease into it slowly so that your body has a chance to adapt to the new demands being placed on it.

CARDIO TRAINING

Strength and power are two key components that can help baseball and softball players on the field. To be a well-rounded athlete, however, cardiovascular training, usually just called "cardio training," is also helpful. Cardio helps to strengthen your heart and lungs as well as train your body to use oxygen more efficiently. These exercises can help build your endurance so that you can play for longer without becoming tired. Some of the best cardio exercises are as simple as running and swimming as well as biking, rowing, and cross-country skiing. All these exercises should be performed for at least thirty minutes at a time to get the full effect.

Again, be sure to take precautions when doing cardio work. Exercises such as running produce repeated impacts against your ankles and knees, so you should be sure to wear the proper footwear and practice the best possible form to lower the risk of injuring these areas of your body. Swimming is one cardio exercise that cushions your joints completely, with much less risk of injury than other forms of cardio activity. In addition, depending on the stroke you use and your range of motion, swimming can greatly improve your flexibility.

Swimming is a great cardio exercise that players can do that puts no stress on the body's joints.

TEXT-DEPENDENT QUESTIONS:

1. What is the movement most used in the games of baseball and softball?

2. Name three guidelines for young pitchers by the American Sports Medicine Institute.

3. What is the goal of weight training?

RESEARCH PROJECT:

Look into what is required to put together an effective off-season training program. What types of non-baseball activities are best to keep players in game shape? How might off-season training vary by position?

WORDS TO UNDERSTAND:

brunt: the main force or stress (such as of an attack)

ligament: a tough piece of tissue in the body that holds bones together or keeps an organ in place

paralysis: a condition in which you are unable to move or feel all or a part of your body

Chapter 4

TAKING CARE OF THE BODY: INJURIES AND NUTRITION

Baseball and softball players suffer more injuries as a whole than players in either football or hockey, which are violent contact sports. This is due to the fact that more kids play baseball and softball than either of those other sports. The percentage of players who get hurt on the diamond is actually relatively low, but injuries do occur, mostly from being hit by the ball.

The CPSC reports that more than 100,000 baseball and softball-related injuries are treated in emergency rooms in the United States annually. There are also thousands of lesser injuries, such as bruises, cuts, and sprains, which are treated with first aid by a coach, another player, or a parent.

Most baseball and softball injuries occur from being hit by the ball.

Warming up, wearing the proper, well-maintained equipment, and maintaining focus throughout workouts, practices, and games are all ways that injury risk can be reduced. The fast action of the game, however, ensures that injuries will happen sometimes, even from the simplest plays, such as throwing the ball or rounding a base. The most important thing is to not ignore the pain so that you can receive immediate treatment and determine whether the injury is serious.

The throwing motion-related joints take the **brunt** of the punishment in baseball and softball. Injuries to the shoulders and arms are expectedly common because players make so many throws. Injuries also occur to the head, knees, and ankles when players collide, runners slide into bases, and fielders dive to make catches. Fractures are common, and many different bones, from fingertips to legs, are cracked, shattered, or broken.

Pitchers are the players most likely to get rotator cuff tears or tendonitis.

SHOULDER AND ARM

The shoulder is the most frequently injured joint in baseball and softball. During a professional baseball season, about one-third of the players on the disabled list have shoulder injuries, and in some years these have caused a total of 6,000 missed days of play. The injury is often described as tendonitis, inflammation, or a strain, and it is an overuse injury caused by throwing the ball over and over. As a result, shoulder pain may come and go for a while and then become progressively worse. Tendonitis means inflammation and pain in the tendons, those tough, fibrous tissues that connect muscles to bones. Baseball players, especially pitchers, often get rotator cuff tendonitis when the tendon tears by rubbing the under part of the shoulder. The rotator cuff is the capsule of tendons and muscles that surround the upper arm and holds the shoulder together. Injuries cause pain on the outside of the shoulder, with pain and weakness when lifting the arm.

> We get so focused on radar gun speeds and velocity. It's important for us to focus on 'now we're throwing harder, we have to make our arm stronger.' Watch the amount of pitches you throw, the amount of innings you throw.
>
> — Roy Halladay, two-time Cy Young award winner

Pain is your friend. When we experience pain, that is the body trying to protect itself from doing more harm.

Shoulder pain, especially in young players, should not be ignored because the stress of throwing can damage the cartilage when growth occurs. A player can even fracture the growth plate in the shoulder or suffer a shoulder separation, a serious **ligament** tear in which the end of the collar bone, or clavicle, rises up. Any of these problems require X-rays and can be treated successfully by rest from the game, physical therapy, or in the worst cases, minor surgery.

SIDEBAR

Tommy John Surgery

Tommy John was a pitcher in the 1970s who suffered a ruptured ulnar collateral ligament (UCL) in his throwing elbow. Dr. Frank Jobe, an orthopedic surgeon working with John's team, the LA Dodgers, developed a technique to reconstruct the ligament with a donor tendon and first performed the operation on John. The operation was wildly successful, and John went on to pitch another fourteen seasons (three of those all-star seasons) and won 164 games post-surgery.

Today, the procedure is relatively common. More than 140 MLB players have had the procedure. In 2015 alone, 20 MLB players had their (UCLs) reconstructed. In the last 20 years, however, there has been an alarming increase in the number of teenagers requiring the surgery. From 2003 to 2014, the number of fifteen- to nineteen-year-olds requiring Tommy John surgery went up more than 300 percent, numbering in the thousands. Common wisdom had been that the injury was caused by throwing certain types of pitches, but a 2002 study demonstrated that pitch volume was much more to blame than pitch type. Kids who throw more than 200 pitches a year have a 63 percent higher chance of injuring the UCL than kids who throw fewer than 200. At 400 pitches, the number jumps to 181 percent.

These findings have led youth baseball leagues to institute strict pitch count monitoring, yet experts project the number of surgeries will continue to rise through 2025.

The joints related to throwing the ball are the ones most likely to be injured in baseball and softball.

The elbow is the other joint susceptible to stress damage caused by constant throwing. It is important to recognize the symptoms early (symptoms include a twinge, tightening, or burning sensation in the muscle). Little League elbow occurs just below the elbow at the inside top of the arm bone, an area of bone that is not yet completely hardened in young players. Often the cartilage is also injured, which can harm the proper movement of the joint throughout life. This is why Little League has limits on the number of throws a pitcher can make (two hundred a week or ninety in a game) and also tries to limit pitchers throwing the curveball because this motion snaps the elbow down. An injured elbow must be X-rayed, and treatment includes rest, icing, compression, and elevation (the R.I.C.E. program) of the injured area. If a pitcher gets Little League elbow, he or she may have to rest the arm for six to eight weeks or until the pain goes away. A pitcher may still play other positions and bat if this does not cause pain. Cartilage damage requires a longer period of rest and medication, and surgery is sometimes needed.

HEAD AND NECK

Being hit by the ball is the most common cause of injuries to the head and, less often, the neck. The CPSC studied 88,700 injuries from being hit by a ball and found that 29.5 percent of the injuries were to the head and neck. Players can also injure these areas by colliding or sliding into a base. The most dangerous head injury is a concussion, which is an injury to the brain that might cause a player to lose memory, be unconscious, or in rare cases, die. Symptoms include a severe headache, nausea, or confusion. If a batter's helmet is damaged by a throw, the force involved could also be enough to cause a concussion. A player who is unconscious should be taken quickly to the doctor. Depending on the severity of the concussion, players will have to skip play for a minimum of seventy-two hours to about one month. Neck injuries include those in which the nerves are stretched, causing temporary numbness and a stinging pain (hence this injury's nickname, "stinger").

Much more serious is the possible neck fracture or spinal injury. Only qualified emergency personnel should move a player who is lying on the ground with a serious neck injury because movement could cause **paralysis** or death. Treatment for minor injuries will require a neck collar or brace, followed by exercise to strengthen the neck.

Lower body injuries to the knees and ankles are common in baseball and softball.

KNEE AND ANKLE

The knee is such an integral part of all movements on the diamond that injuries to the joint can occur at any time. The knee's connecting tissues can be stretched or torn by a runner turning or sliding, a fielder twisting for a fly ball, or a pitcher making a delivery. A sprain is a partial or complete tear of a ligament, while a strain is the same injury to a muscle or tendon. You will know you have a sprained or strained knee if you hear a popping or snapping sound, feel pain from inside the knee, and are unable to put weight on that leg—or if you feel that your knee is loose. The R.I.C.E. treatment will help, and players with severe injuries may have to use a splint or crutches for a while.

In some cases, a small piece of cartilage breaks off from the end of the bone. You will be unable to extend the leg. Other symptoms are pain, swelling, stiffness, and a catching sensation when you move. A physician will insist that you rest the knee and wear a cast for about two months. Sometimes surgery is necessary.

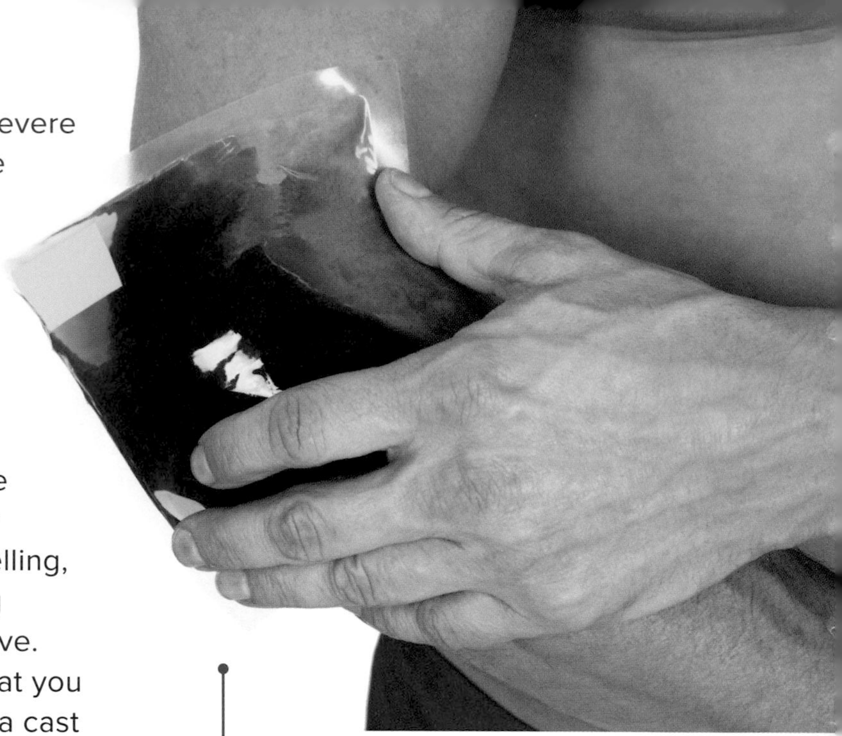

Icing a sore elbow after a game is effective at reducing pain and swelling.

Baseball and softball players often suffer ankle sprains. Most twisted ankles are usually minor sprains that may not require treatment, but a team trainer or physician should tape serious sprains. If the ankle is rested, a player can return to competition within days, but if the injury is ignored, recovery could take weeks or months. Treatment is the usual R.I.C.E. program, an ankle brace or tape, and perhaps crutches. Inflammation lasts about three days, and exercises to strengthen the ankle can begin when the player can move without pain.

R.I.C.E.

Rest, ice, compression, and elevation is a treatment program most often applied to sprains and strains. The following steps should take place twenty-four to forty-eight hours after an injury.

- **Rest**. Do not use the injured area; this may even mean bed rest. Serious injuries, such as a broken arm, require immobilization (usually with a cast) for a short period. The time needed for rest varies, depending on the injury.

- **Ice**. Put ice on the injured area as soon as possible. This is effective in the first two or three days. Apply ice two or three times an hour for twelve to twenty minutes each time. Use an ice pack or crushed ice in a plastic bag. Never put ice directly against the skin; wrap the ice in a towel, and keep it in place with a bandage—or place a thin piece of cotton between the ice and the skin.
- **Compression**. Wrap an elastic bandage snugly around the injured area, being careful not to wrap it tight enough to cut off blood flow.
- **Elevation**. Raise the injured area above your heart level, if possible. You can use pillows as props.

NUTRITION

Baseball is not a sport that requires endurance and stamina. For most players, there are long periods of inactivity that are broken up by short bursts of explosive action. Therefore baseball and softball players must be especially careful to eat a balanced diet.

WHAT TO EAT

While a balanced diet is important for everyone, it is even more important for athletes. Typically, an athlete has to eat considerably more than other

Baseball and softball players should eat about 3,000 calories while training or in season.

people do. The United States Food and Drug Administration (FDA) suggests that the average American should eat about 2,000 calories a day; for a male high school- or college-level baseball player, a 3,000- to 4,000-calorie diet is more common. There are three main food groups to consider when choosing a diet: carbohydrates, protein, and fats.

Learn in-season nutrition tips from three-time MLB all-star 3B Evan Longoria.

CARBOHYDRATES

Carbohydrates are foods rich in a chemical called starch, which is what the body breaks down to get energy. Starchy foods include breads and grains, vegetables such as potatoes, cereal, pasta, and rice. There is no one-size-fits-all formula that can exactly dictate what an athlete's carb consumption should be. A general rule is that in season or during times of intense training, athletes should eat about 5 grams (0.2 ounces) of carbs for every pound (0.5 kilogram) of body weight. In the off-season or during periods of lower training levels, it should be about 2 to 3 grams (0.07–0.10 ounces) per pound. The body

Simple carbs like those in white bread are quickly broken down into sugars and should be avoided by athletes.

uses carbs strictly for fuel, so if they are not being burned, they are turned into fat and stored. Therefore it is important to adjust carb intake based on activity level. Athletes should not eat heavily processed carbohydrates such as white sugar and white flour. These simple carbs are quickly broken down into sugars, which the body processes into fats if it does not immediately burn them off. The best carbohydrate choices for an athlete are complex types like pasta and whole grain foods as well as starchy vegetables. A nutritious diet avoids empty calories or those provided by food that lacks other nourishment, like processed sugar and starches.

PROTEIN

Unlike carbohydrates, protein is used within the body. Proteins are important chemicals used to perform specific functions inside our body's cells. Our bodies can break down proteins that are found in foods and use them to build new proteins that make up our muscles and bones. During periods of intense training and activity, the body needs more protein to repair damage to muscles. Not eating enough protein can cause an athlete to lose muscle mass and negatively affect the ability to perform. The Academy of Nutrition and Dietetics recommends athletes consume about 0.50 to 0.75 gram (0.02–0.03 ounces) of protein for every pound (0.5 kilogram) of body weight. During the season or heavy training, that number should be closer to a full gram (0.04 ounces) per pound. This higher ratio is also true if an athlete is trying to build muscle mass. The best sources of proteins are lean meats and dairy products (such as milk or cheese) as well as eggs and certain types of soy, beans, and nuts.

The best sources of proteins are meats and dairy products, such as milk or cheese as well as eggs and beans.

Fats from processed foods are high in bad cholesterol and should be avoided.

FATS

Lots of times, we think of fats as bad for us because eating too much of them is unhealthy. However, fat is an important ingredient needed to make our bodies work correctly. They help balance hormone production, support cell growth, and protect our organs, among other functions. Without fats, our bodies cannot absorb certain vitamins as well as they should. Also, our skin and hair need some amount of fat to grow correctly. However, fat should still be eaten in moderation as it is higher in calories than protein or carbs. No more than 70 grams (2.5 ounces) a day is recommended. All fats are not created equal, however. Trans fats and saturated fats found in processed foods are high in bad cholesterol, which clogs arteries and is bad for the heart. The best sources of fat are vegetable oils, olive oil, and nuts.

DIETARY SUPPLEMENTS

Ideally, a balanced diet would provide our bodies with all the nutrients it needs. However, due to many varying factors, eating optimally is not always possible. Dietary supplements are available to fill dietary gaps created by a deficient diet.

In discussing dietary supplements here, this does not include banned performance-enhancing substances. Instead, the focus is on supplements that contain vitamins, minerals, and other compounds that help the body absorb nutrients or recover more efficiently. When properly used supplements can improve overall health and performance, but you should always consult a doctor or other expert before using them to augment your diet or training program. Some examples of common supplements include vitamin tablets and protein shakes or powder.

VITAMIN TABLETS

For many reasons, we do not always get the vitamins and nutrients we need. Often, this is because our diets are not as balanced as they should be. Sometimes, it is because the foods that are available to us have been processed in such a way that they lose nutrients. If you know or suspect that a certain key vitamin is underrepresented in what you are eating, in many cases, the necessary vitamins can be obtained from vitamin supplements. These supplements, which are usually taken as a pill, can either contain a balanced mixture of vitamins and nutrients (multivitamins) or contain a single vitamin or mineral that our diet is lacking. The best way to avoid this issue is to work hard to eat right whenever possible.

PROTEIN SUPPLEMENTS

Getting enough protein from the food you eat can be difficult as well. For athletes, eating protein immediately after a workout is recommended (to refuel the body), but most people either don't feel up to or do not have the time to spend cooking or preparing themselves a meal immediately after a workout. That is where protein shakes come in handy. These are a protein supplement sold in powder form that look and taste like milkshakes when blended with water but contain no dairy products. Protein shakes deliver a high ratio of protein to carbohydrates and calories. They are not meant to replace meals. Many other necessary nutrients are gained from a balanced diet that cannot be replaced by protein shakes, regardless of how fortified they may be.

Powdered protein supplements are a quick and easy way to get a pre- or post-workout protein boost.

STAYING HYDRATED

The body needs water more than it needs any other nutrient. If you are not getting enough water, your performance will suffer in spite of any preparation or balanced diet. Dehydration occurs when your body doesn't have enough water. Symptoms include fatigue, dizziness, and headaches. No athlete can perform at his or her best if not properly hydrated. Proper hydration should be maintained not only at games but throughout training as well. The body does not store water, so we need to constantly maintain its supply. The American College of Sports Medicine recommends these guidelines for athletes:

- **Before Exercise:** Drink 16 to 20 ounces (473–591 milliliters) within the two-hour period prior to exercise.
- **During Exercise:** Drink 4 to 8 ounces (118–237 milliliters) every fifteen to twenty minutes during exercise.
- **Post Exercise:** Replace 24 ounces (710 milliliters) for every pound (0.5 kilogram) of body weight lost during exercise.

Baseball and softball are summer sports played mostly outdoors in the full heat of the summer. Players will need to drink more than the recommended amount on hot days when they are sweating heavily. Be sure to have plenty of water on hand. A low-calorie sports drink is also a good idea to replace electrolytes lost through sweating.

Players should have water handy on the bench or in the dugout to stay hydrated, especially during games played in hot weather.

TEXT-DEPENDENT QUESTIONS:

1. What is the most frequently injured joint in baseball and softball?

2. What are three main food groups to consider when choosing a diet?

3. What kind of shakes delivers a high ratio of protein to carbohydrates and calories?

RESEARCH PROJECT:

Put together a sample nutrition plan for yourself by mapping out meals and snacks for a given week. Pick a week when you are training and competing. Be sure to consider the nutrition benefits of everything you choose as well as the time it will take to make the plan work in your busy schedule. Don't forget to include a hydration schedule.

WORDS TO UNDERSTAND:

generated: to produce (something) or cause (something) to be produced

prolific: producing a large amount of something

strike zone: the area over home plate through which a pitched baseball must pass to be called a strike

Chapter 5

BASEBALL AND SOFTBALL: FROM SANDLOTS TO STADIUMS AND FOREIGN SHORES

OF BATS, BALLS, BOXING GLOVES, AND BABE RUTH

The game of baseball was not invented by any one person at any certain time. Baseball evolved from numerous forms of stick and ball games over the course of several centuries. Accounts of similar sounding games exist that date back 3,000 years.

Baseball came to America in the eighteenth century. It existed in as many different varieties as there were immigrant communities that played their version of the sport. The bat and the ball were the common denominators. Rules were not formally derived until 1845. That year, Alexander Cartwright formed a team to represent his Knickerbocker Club in New York and decided to write down formal rules, which included the following:

Baseball in America is as old as the United States itself, but formal rules were not developed until 1845.

In the early days of baseball, throwing the ball at them, rather than tagging them with it, put out base runners.

- Establishing which portions of the field were fair versus foul territory
- Setting the distance between bases at thirty paces
- Tagging runners with the ball to get them out rather than throwing it at them

Establishing these set parameters made Cartwright the founder of the modern game. The rules continued to evolve over the next few decades. The three strike or four ball standard for an at bat was established. In 1877, the distance between the bases was set at the much more consistent distance of ninety feet (twenty-seven meters). Pitchers actually threw underhand until 1884.

By 1887, baseball in various forms and varieties had been developing and evolving in America for more than a century. That year, the game now considered to be baseball's sister sport came about, but surprisingly, the idea for softball did not derive from baseball directly.

Softball came about because of a football game. The story tells of a Thanksgiving Day gathering of Yale and Harvard University alumni at a boat club in Chicago. The group awaited news of that day's football game between the two schools. When the telegraph came revealing that Yale won, a Yale supporter tossed a boxing glove at a Harvard alumnus, who swung at it with the handle end of a broom, and "indoor baseball" was born. They drew a chalk diamond on the floor and tied the boxing glove into a ball. The group of Farragut Boat Club members, led by George Hancock, devised rules for the game, which then quickly spread throughout the Midwest, going by names such as "mush ball" and "kitten baseball." Hancock, a reporter by trade, wrote and published rules for the game called the Indoor Baseball Guide. The game moved outdoors in the spring of 1888, and Hancock published a set of indoor/outdoor rules in 1889.

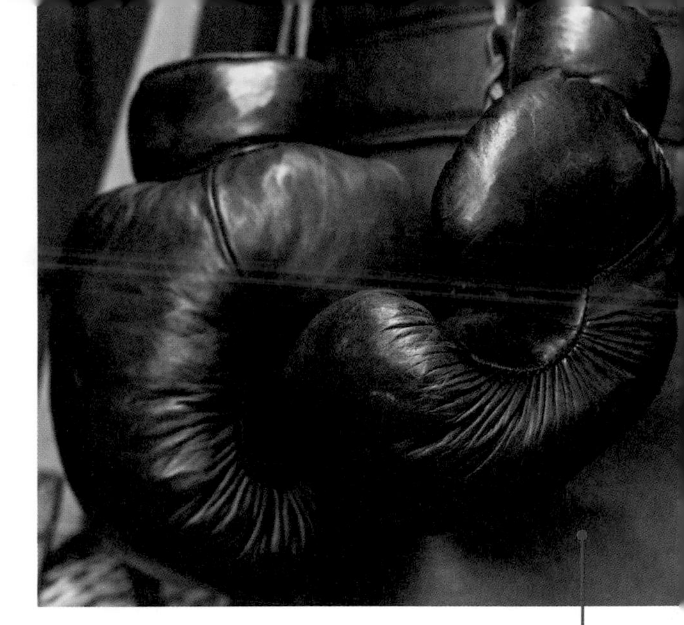

The very first softball was actually just a boxing glove tied into a ball with string.

The term "softball" was first attributed to Walter Hakanson, an official at the YMCA in Denver, who suggested it to the rules committee at a National Recreation Congress meeting in 1926. Four years later, the name "softball" was official. Official rules for an organized sport were drawn up in 1934. One of the major changes was going from the sixteen-inch (forty-one-centimeter) ball that replaced the original rolled-up boxing glove to a twelve-inch (thirty-centimeter) ball, which is still the sport's official ball size. In Chicago today, however, true to the original version, you can still find games of "mush ball," played with a sixteen-inch ball and players without gloves.

The current seventeen-inch (forty-three-centimeter) wide pentagonal home plate was implemented in the National League in 1900.

Babe Ruth led the Red Sox to victory in the 1918 World Series, the last the team would win for eighty-six years.

By the mid-1930s, baseball was the most popular sport in the country. The rules, which now included the pitching rubber at sixty feet and six inches (eighteen meters) from the now familiar five-sided plate, had been constant since 1900. In the three decades since, baseball went from a ragtag collection of leagues that staged games marred by violence on the field and in the stands to a professional sport with two stable leagues and a championship in the World Series that was the biggest sporting event in the United States. This was in no small part due to one player, George "Babe" Ruth.

Ruth began his MLB career as a pitcher with the Boston Red Sox, joining them after a transfer from his minor league team on July 11, 1914, at age nineteen. That year he was up and down to the minors, pitching just four games and getting just two hits at the plate. In his second season Ruth was with the Sox full time, winning eighteen of his twenty-eight starts and helping Boston reach the World Series, where they lost. The 1916 and 1917 seasons saw Ruth establish himself as one of the best pitchers in the American League (AL), winning more than twenty games each season. In 1916 he led the AL in starts, shutouts, and earned run average (ERA) and led the Sox to the World Series again. In the World Series, he pitched one game, a complete game, fourteen-inning, six-hit victory in game two, and Boston beat Brooklyn in five games.

In May of the 1918 season, Boston manager Ed Barrow gave in to Ruth's request to play in the outfield, so he could hit on days he was not pitching. Ruth hit three home runs that month. That might not sound like much by today's standards, but this was the "dead ball" era. The league leader in home runs hit just nine the previous year. Ruth went on to hit eleven that year to lead the league. Ruth pitched and won two games to help Boston win the 1918 World Series, but his days as a pitcher were numbered. So were his days with Boston.

Despite his success in Boston, Ruth (image at left) is mostly remembered as a New York Yankee great. He is displayed prominently with other Yankee icons in the promenade at the new Yankee Stadium.

In the 1919 season, Ruth pitched just seventeen times but hit an MLB record twenty-nine home runs, shattering the old mark by thirteen. Ruth was the biggest attraction in baseball, which did not go unnoticed by Boston's cash-strapped owner, Harry Frazee. On January 5, 1920, Frazee sold Ruth to the New York Yankees for $100,000, initiating what was known as the "Curse of the Bambino." This curse referred to the Red Sox prospects of winning the World Series, which they did not do for eighty-six years after the deal.

Ruth, of course, went on to have one of the sport's most **prolific** careers with the Yankees. The baseball changed in 1920, and in the first year with the "live ball," Ruth crushed fifty-four home runs. In fifteen seasons with the Yankees, Ruth led the league in home runs ten times (including sixty in 1927), in runs batted in (RBI) four times, and in runs scored seven times. He was the 1923 AL MVP when he hit .393 and led the league in almost every other offensive category. Most importantly, Ruth's Yankees won four World Series.

FASTPITCH, SLOW PITCH, AND JENNIE FINCH

At the time Ruth retired in 1935, softball was coming into its own as a sport. The sport's U.S. governing body, the Amateur Softball Association, was founded in 1933, hundreds of leagues had popped up around the country, and the game was now played mostly outdoors. These leagues were of the fastpitch variety as fastpitch softball began to develop and was the more popular version by 1940. Softball games are only seven innings long in both current versions. Here are the main differences between the fast- and slow pitch versions of the sport, as described by isport.com:

FASTPITCH

- This version is reserved for female athletes. Its players range from five-year-olds who play with rag balls to adults who compete in college or at the professional level.
- The pitching distance can range between thirty-five and forty-three feet (eleven to thirteen meters), depending on the age of the players.
- The pitcher's motion is a full windmill that rotates 360 degrees around her shoulder before it's delivered.
- Pitches are thrown along a straight plane, curving and diving to the left, right, top, and bottom of a **strike zone** that extends from the batter's knees to her chest.
- Bats are regulated to have a thirty-four-inch (eighty-six-centimeter) maximum length with a maximum drop (length minus weight) of twelve.

Fast pitch softball is a women's sport that uses a full windmill arm action to generate speed on pitches.

- Each team has the traditional nine defensive players on the field.
- It requires catchers to wear full protective gear.
- If after five innings one team leads by eight or more runs, the leading team is declared the winner. This is called the "mercy rule."

Watch U.S. Softball Olympian Jennie Finch giving pitching mechanics tips.

SLOW PITCH

- Rules mandate a pitching distance of fifty feet (fifteen meters) for both male and female players.
- The pitcher's wind-up motion is a half windmill.
- The pitch must be thrown with an arc between six to twelve feet (two to four meters) high. If the arc is not high enough, the umpire will call the pitch illegal.
- The pitch must also be lofted in such a way that it falls onto the plate for it to be a called strike.
- There is no bunting.
- An automatic out is called on a two-strike foul ball.

- There is no designated hitter.
- Bats also have a thirty-four-inch (eight-six-centimeter) maximum length, but the maximum weight is thirty-eight ounces (one kilogram).
- There are ten defensive players. The tenth player either plays as a fourth outfielder or acts as a "rover" in the shallow outfield between shortstop and second base.
- Catchers are not required to wear protective gear (although many opt to wear a mask).
- There is no leading off on the base paths.
- There is no base stealing or advancing on passed balls.
- There are no pinch runners.
- There are no metal cleats.
- The mercy rules ends the game if one team takes a fifteen or more run lead after the fourth inning.

The newly formed International Softball Federation (ISF) formally recognized slow pitch in 1952, as did the Amateur Softball Association (ASA) in 1953. Although the ISF, softball's 124-member country international governing body, wrote slow pitch out of its rules in 2002, the sport still thrives in America under the ASA.

Slow-pitch softball is no longer recognized as an international sport, but there are hundreds of leagues in the United States.

In 2016, Carol Hitchins became the most successful head coach in the history of NCAA Division I softball when she coached her Michigan Wolverine's squad in her 1,458th victory. Hitchins has coached at Michigan for more than thirty years, getting into coaching soon after her career as a player at Michigan State ended.

Hitchins's success at Michigan has resulted in a single national championship. The top-ranked Wolverines defeated UCLA two games to one in 2005 to win the Women' College World Series. This was no small accomplishment. Michigan was the first team in the history of the series from east of the Mississippi river to win the championship. The best players tended to go to softball powerhouses like UCLA and Arizona. Couple that with the fact that Michigan played its first thirty-three games on the road due to weather. Hitchins' win showed that Eastern schools could play as well, and Eastern schools Florida and Alabama have since followed Hitchins' success with wins of their own.

Hitchins was inducted into the National Fastpitch Coaches Association Hall of Fame the year after winning the national championship. She has coached twenty-two First Team All-Americans and twice been voted National Fastpitch Coaches Association National Coach of the Year.

It is fastpitch softball that is most commonly referred to in discussions of the sport. This version was added to the roster of summer Olympic sports for the 1996 games in Atlanta. Softball only lasted as an Olympic event through four games, from 1996 to 2008. In that time, the United States won three gold medals and one silver. At the 2004 games in Athens, the Americans surrendered only one run in the entire tournament. Superstar pitcher Jennie Finch had a lot to do with that.

> Focus on correct spin and being able to hit your location. It's better to have a few pitches that actually work.
>
> – Jennie Finch, Olympic gold medalist

In 2004, Finch was already a softball star, having dominated for four seasons at the University of Arizona, striking out more than 1,000 batters from 1999 to 2002. In her junior season in 2001, Finch was undefeated, going 32–0 in thirty-two starts with a 0.54 ERA. The Wildcats won the Women's College World Series, and Finch was named series MVP and National Collegiate Athletic Association (NCAA) Pitcher of the Year. She graduated with several NCAA records, including fifty-one consecutive wins. Her career .881 winning percentage is seventh best all-time.

In 2004, Finch and the Americans were heavily favored as the two-time defending softball champions, and they did not disappoint. In the preliminary round, they outscored opponents 41 to 0. Finch gave up just four hits in the two shutouts she pitched. Teammate Lisa Fernandez pitched the two medal round victories to clinch the gold.

WHOSE PASTIME IS THIS ANYWAY?

Both baseball (also dropped after 2008) and softball will be back at the Olympics but only for the 2020 games in Tokyo, along with karate, sport climbing, surfing, and skateboarding, sports that are popular in Japanese culture.

Softball star Jennie Finch, seen here on the night her team won an ESPY award for Best Female Olympic Performance after winning the Olympic gold medal in 2004.

Baseball has been popular in Japan since the nineteenth century. An American professor from Maine named Horace Wilson introduced the game to his students while teaching at what is now Tokyo Imperial University in the early 1870s. By the time he returned to America in 1877, baseball had a loyal following in Tokyo. The first organized teams and leagues were all formed prior to 1900, and the first professional league debuted in 1936. In 1950, Nippon Professional Baseball (NPB) was founded, which is now the very popular twelve-team league known as Puro Yakyu. The NPB has **generated** some very high-quality players, many of whom have played in America.

The Japanese are enthusiastic and passionate baseball fans.

In 1964 and 1965, twenty-year-old Masanori Murakami became the first Japanese player to play in the American Major Leagues. He pitched in fifty-four games, fifty-three as a reliever, going 5–1 with a 3.43 ERA before returning to Japan. Thirty years later, twenty-six-year-old NPB superstar pitcher Hideo Nomo famously signed with the Los Angeles Dodgers to pave the way for modern-day Japanese players to play in America. Since Nomo, more than fifty Japanese players have played in MLB, none better than Ichiro Suzuki.

Ichiro did not debut in the majors until he was twenty-seven. Already a superstar in Japan, he signed with Seattle in 2001 after setting NPB single-season records for hits and batting average. The rookie got 242 hits in his debut season with Seattle, leading the league in hitting at .350 and stolen bases with fifty-six. He was named to the all-star team and won a Gold Glove in center field, Rookie of the Year, and AL MVP. He won ten straight Gold Gloves and made ten straight all-star teams to start his MLB career. Ichiro has surpassed two hundred hits in a season ten times, leading the league seven times, including an MLB record 262 in 2004. In 2016 he collected his 3,000th career hit, something only twenty-nine others have done. If he had played his first nine seasons in the majors instead of Japan, Ichiro would likely have in the neighborhood of 4,300 hits. That would be the most in history. Only Pete Rose and Ty Cobb have more than 3,800 career hits.

Ichiro is just one great example of how international the sport has become. In 2015, 26.5 percent of MLB players were born outside of the United States. Here are the top five birthplaces:

In 2016, as a member of the Miami Marlins, Ichiro Suzuki got career hit number 3,000.

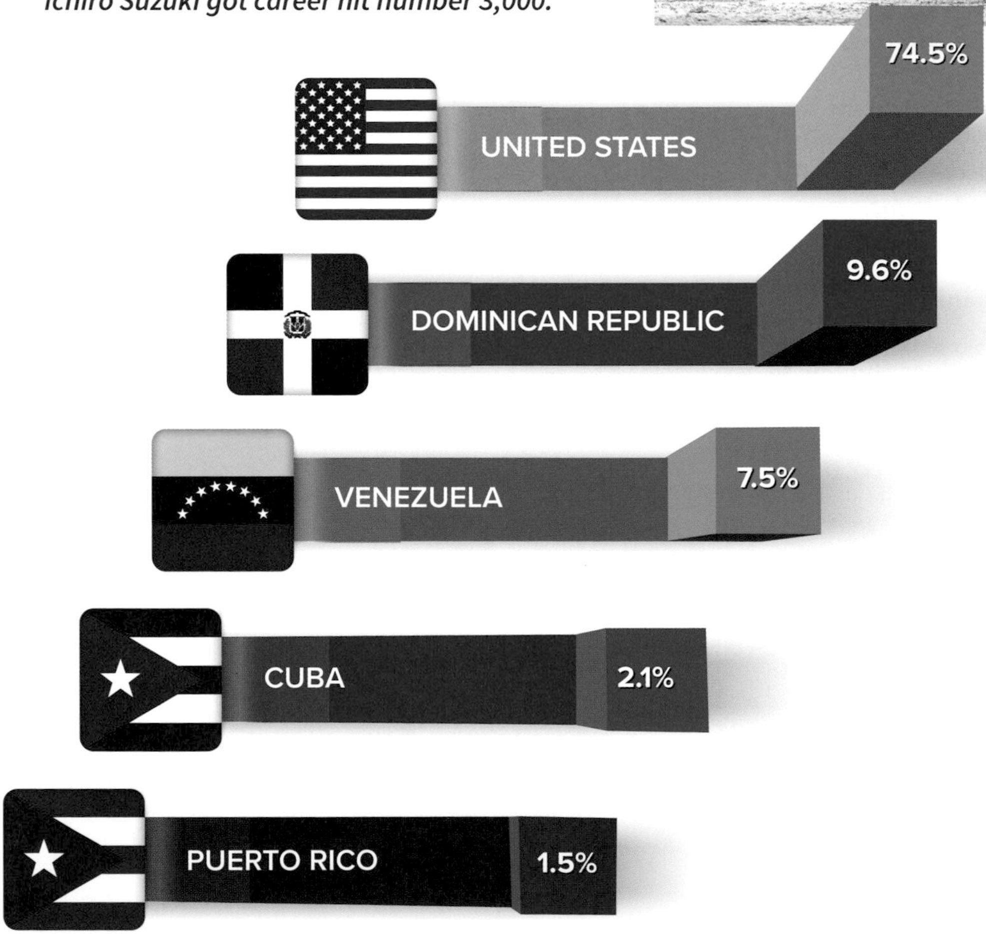

UNITED STATES 74.5%

DOMINICAN REPUBLIC 9.6%

VENEZUELA 7.5%

CUBA 2.1%

PUERTO RICO 1.5%

Japan is actually sixth at just over 1 percent. What this demonstrates is how much Latin American countries (and Puerto Rico) love baseball. Every year players from these countries represent a larger share of the player pool, and that is a trend that is likely to continue.

It is not only that more people in baseball-loving countries are playing baseball, but it is also that fewer people in the United States love playing baseball. A 2015 study from the Sports and Fitness Industry Association showed that 300,000 fewer kids between six and seventeen years old were playing organized baseball in 2014 than in 2009 (fastpitch softball was actually up slightly over the same time period). That is half the decline seen in youth football, but the football decline is not surprising, given the high-profile concussion concerns with that sport.

In the Dominican Republic, despite limited resources, baseball is a popular and thriving sport.

The problem may be that baseball is just not as interesting to kids as other sports options. Consider that on any given play, a fielder has only about a 10 percent chance of being involved, on average. Hitters swing and miss 70 percent of the time, and scoring is generally low in today's game. If you have been to a youth baseball game, you know there is a lot of standing around. So what are some possible solutions?

Focus on training—a USA Baseball study showed that in areas with skill camps, participation increased 10 percent. If the camp was affiliated with a high-profile person or organization, participation jumped 200 percent.

Fun, fun, fun—Keeping kids engaged at practice means they will enjoy learning more. Coaches should run practices where as many kids are touching a ball or swinging a bat as possible.

Radical rules—Hall of Fame shortstop Cal Ripken Jr. is a special advisor to the MLB commissioner on youth programs and outreach. In 2016, he proposed some unconventional ideas to get kids interested in baseball again:

- Starting every inning with a runner on first base
- Starting each inning with a different count
- Requiring players to steal
- Switching from three outs an inning to five batters

Some have taken issue with these ideas as concessions to the short attention span of today's kids instead of addressing the issue of having the right training for coaches, the theory being that a good teacher can make any subject interesting.

The fact is that the great American pastime has fallen behind other more popular team sports, and if baseball is once again to become a game with mass appeal, something will need to be done to speak to a generation of young people happily growing up without it.

Hall of Fame shortstop Cal Ripken Jr. has ideas on how to make baseball more fun for kids.

TEXT-DEPENDENT QUESTIONS:

1. The term “softball” is first attributed to whom?
2. Name five main differences between the fast- and slow pitch versions of softball.
3. A 2015 study from the Sports and Fitness Industry Association showed that how many fewer kids between six and seventeen years old were playing organized baseball in 2014 than in 2009?

RESEARCH PROJECT:

Think of three things about baseball that you would change if you could. Come up with a hypothesis about the impact you think your changes would have on the sport. Do some research to find information to support or refute your theory.

SERIES GLOSSARY OF KEY TERMS

Acute Injury: Usually the result of a specific impact or traumatic event that occurs in one specific area of the body, such as a muscle, bone, or joint.

Calories: units of heat used to indicate the amount of energy that foods will produce in the human body.

Carbohydrates: substances found in certain foods (such as bread, rice, and potatoes) that provide the body with heat and energy and are made of carbon, hydrogen, and oxygen.

Cardiovascular: of or relating to the heart and blood vessels.

Concussion: a stunning, damaging, or shattering effect from a hard blow—especially a jarring injury of the brain resulting in a disturbance of cerebral function.

Confidence: faith in oneself and one's abilities without any suggestion of conceit or arrogance.

Cooldown: easy exercise, done after more intense activity, to allow the body to gradually transition to a resting or near-resting state.

Dietary Supplements: products taken orally that contain one or more ingredient (such as vitamins or amino acids) that are intended to supplement one's diet and are not considered food.

Dynamic: having active strength of body or mind.

Electrolytes: substances (such as sodium or calcium) that are ions in the body regulating the flow of nutrients into and waste products out of cells.

Flexible: applies to something that can be readily bent, twisted, or folded without any sign of injury.

Hamstrings: any of three muscles at the back of the thigh that function to flex and rotate the leg and extend the thigh.

Hydration: to supply with ample fluid or moisture.

Imagery: mental images, the products of imagination.

Mind-Set: a mental attitude or inclination.

Overuse Injury: an injury that is most likely to occur to the ankles, knees, hands, and wrists, due to the excessive use of these body parts during exercise and athletics.

Plyometrics: also known as "jump training" or "plyos," exercises in which muscles exert maximum force in short intervals of time, with the goal of increasing power (speed and strength).

Positive Mental Attitude (PMA): the philosophy that having an optimistic disposition in every situation in one's life attracts positive changes and increases achievement.

Protein: a nutrient found in food (as in meat, milk, eggs, and beans) that is made up of many amino acids joined together, is a necessary part of the diet, and is essential for normal cell structure and function.

Quadriceps: the greater extensor muscle of the front of the thigh that is divided into four parts.

Recovery: the act or process of becoming healthy after an illness or injury.

Resistance: relating to exercise, involving pushing against a source of resistance (such as a weight) to increase strength. Strength training, or resistance exercises, are those that build muscle. They create stronger and larger muscles by producing more and tougher muscle fibers to cope with the increasing weight demands.

Strategy: a careful plan or method.

Stretching: to extend one's body or limbs from a cramped, stooping, or relaxed position.

Tactics: actions or methods that are planned and used to achieve a particular goal.

Tendon: a tough piece of tissue in the body that connects a muscle to a bone.

Training: the process by which an athlete prepares for competition by exercising, practicing, and so on.

Warm-Up: exercise or practice especially before a game or contest—broadly, to get ready.

Workout: a practice or exercise to test or improve one's fitness for athletic competition, ability, or performance.

FURTHER READING:

Rogers, Paul. *The Athlete's Guide to Stretching: Increasing Flexibility for Injury Prevention and Rehabilitation (Sports Science Book 1).* Seattle, WA: Amazon Digital Services LLC, 2015.

Hinnant, Jama. *Top 10 Injuries in Baseball (Sports Greats).* New York, NY: Enslow Publishing, 2016.

Correa, Joseph. *Infinite Energy in Baseball: Unlocking Your Resting Metabolic Rate to Reduce Injuries, Have More Energy, and Increase Concentration Levels During Competition.* CreateSpace Independent Publishing, 2016.

Luke, Andrew. *Baseball (Inside the World of Sports).* Broomall, PA: Mason Crest, 2017.

INTERNET RESOURCES:

Stop Sports Injuries: ***http://www.stopsportsinjuries.org/STOP/Prevent_Injuries/Baseball_Injury_Prevention.aspx***

The American Sports Medicine Institute: ***http://www.asmi.org/***

FDA: Dietary Supplements:
http://www.fda.gov/Food/DietarySupplements/default.htm

Major League Baseball: ***http://mlb.mlb.com/home***

VIDEO CREDITS:

Pros discuss pregame hitting drills: ***http://x-qr.net/1FkX***

Texas A&M two-time All-American Amanda Scarborough talks about the mental approach to an at bat: ***http://x-qr.net/1FGo***

Players at the University of California–Berkley work on strength and conditioning: ***http://x-qr.net/1CwQ***

Learn in-season nutrition tips from three-time MLB all-Star 3B Evan Longoria: ***http://x-qr.net/1Hg8***

Watch U.S. Softball Olympian Jennie Finch giving pitching mechanic tips: ***http://x-qr.net/1F5Y***

14

PICTURE CREDITS

Page: 3, 5, 17, 27, 41, 55, 71, 80: Skoreya/Shutterstock.com; 6: Eugene Onischenko/Shutterstock.com; 8: Pavel Siamionau I Dreamstime.com; 9: Barbara Helgason I Dreamstime.com; 10: Pro Baseball Insider/youtube.com; 11: Chad Mcdermott I Dreamstime.com; 12: Danhowl I Dreamstime.com; 14: Scott Anderson I Dreamstime.com; 15: Derrick Neill I Dreamstime.com; 16: Eric Broder Van Dyke I Dreamstime.com; 17, 27, 41, 55, 71: Bjoern Wylezich/Shutterstock.com; 18: Ljupco Smokovski/Shutterstock.com; 19, 62: Jamie Roach I Dreamstime.com; 20: All TeamExpress/youtube.com; 21: Rob Corbett I Dreamstime.com; 22: Bcnewell I Dreamstime.com, Aspenphoto I Dreamstime.com; 23: Americanspirit I Dreamstime.com; 24: Prairierattler I Dreamstime.com; 26: Thomaskelley I Dreamstime.com, Scott Anderson I Dreamstime.com; 28: John Kershner/Shutterstock.com; 29: Mary Katherine Wynn I Dreamstime.com; 30: Dan Fleckner I Dreamstime.com; 31: Faberr Ink/Shutterstock.com, Jeffrey Williams I Dreamstime.com; 34: Macrovector/Shutterstock.com, Aspenphoto I Dreamstime.com; 35: Kim Reinick I Dreamstime.com; 37: Cal Bears/youtube.com; 38: Csproductions I Dreamstime.com; 40: Chris Schmid I Dreamstime.com; 42: Daxiao Productions/Shutterstock.com; 43: Susan Leggett I Dreamstime.com; 44: Glen Jones I Dreamstime.com; 45, 65: Florian Augustin/Shutterstock.com; 46: Angelina Scully I Dreamstime.com; 47: Aspenphoto I Dreamstime.com; 48: Andrey Popov I Dreamstime.com; 49: Olgany I Dreamstime.com; 50: newbalance/youtube.com, Tmarqua I Dreamstime.com; 51: Robyn Mackenzie I Dreamstime.com; 52: Karin Hildebrand Lau I Dreamstime.com; 53: Itm20 I Dreamstime.com; 54: Allenfive5 I Dreamstime.com; 56: Jamie Roach/Shutterstock.com; 57: Michael Flippo I Dreamstime.com; 58: Mbr Images I Dreamstime.com; 59: Baloncici I Dreamstime.com, Chris Hill I Dreamstime.com; 60, 68, 70: Jerry Coli I Dreamstime.com; 61: David Leindecker I Dreamstime.com; 63: ASL Productions/youtube.com; 64: García Juan I Dreamstime.com; 66: Sbukley I Dreamstime.com; 67: James Kirkikis I Dreamstime.com; 68: My Life Graphic/Shutterstock.com, Olha Insight/Shutterstock.com; 69: Stefano Ember I Dreamstime.com; 75: Will Hughes/Shutterstock.com

Chapter number illustrations: Alhovik/Shutterstock.com
Quote bubbles: Mr Aesthetics/Shutterstock.com
Video player: Mauro Fabbro/Shutterstock.com

QR CODES AND LINKS TO THIRD-PARTY CONTENT

You may gain access to certain third-party content ("Third-Party Sites") by scanning and using the QR Codes that appear in this publication (the "QR Codes"). We do not operate or control in any respect any information, products, or services on such Third-Party Sites linked to by us via the QR Codes included in this publication, and we assume no responsibility for any materials you may access using the QR Codes. Your use of the QR Codes may be subject to terms, limitations, or restrictions set forth in the applicable terms of use or otherwise established by the owners of the Third-Party Sites. Our linking to such Third-Party Sites via the QR Codes does not imply an endorsement or sponsorship of such Third-Party Sites or the information, products, or services offered on or through the Third-Party Sites, nor does it imply an endorsement or sponsorship of this publication by the owners of such Third-Party Sites.

INDEX

In this index, page numbers in ***bold italics*** font indicate photos or videos.

ABOUT THE AUTHOR

Peter Douglas is a former journalist, reporting on both sports and general news for many years at television stations in various locations across the US affiliated with NBC, CBS and Fox. Prior to his journalism career he worked with the Boston Red Sox Major League baseball team. An avid writer and sports enthusiast, he has authored 16 additional books on sports topics. In his downtime Peter enjoys family time with his wife and two young children and attending hockey and baseball games in his home city.